THIS FOX
—AND—
THAT FOX

BY LINDA LOTT
ILLUSTRATED BY WENDY RASMUSSEN

PEARSON

Scott
Foresman

Editorial Offices: Glenview, Illinois • Parsippany, New Jersey • New York, New York
Sales Offices: Needham, Massachusetts • Duluth, Georgia • Glenview, Illinois
Coppell, Texas • Ontario, California • Mesa, Arizona

This is a fox.

She eats little animals.

She is in the woods.

This is a fox too.

She is in the zoo.

We like watching her.

She is looking back.

We see her sit.

This is a fox.

She is in the town.

She is looking for her dinner.

This fox is in the zoo.

Sam has dinner for her.

We can watch her eat.

This is a fox.

That is a fox.

See where they live.